YOUR KNOWLEDGE HAS

- We will publish your bachelor's and
  master's thesis, essays and papers

- Your own eBook and book -
  sold worldwide in all relevant shops

- Earn money with each sale

Upload your text at www.GRIN.com
and publish for free

Mohamed Rahama

Data Mining - a search for knowledge

GRIN Verlag

Bibliografische Information der Deutschen Nationalbibliothek:

Die Deutsche Bibliothek verzeichnet diese Publikation in der Deutschen National-
bibliografie; detaillierte bibliografische Daten sind im Internet über http://dnb.d-
nb.de/ abrufbar.

Imprint:

Copyright © 2012 GRIN Verlag GmbH
Druck und Bindung: Books on Demand GmbH, Norderstedt Germany
ISBN: 978-3-656-29603-4

This book at GRIN:

http://www.grin.com/en/e-book/201604/data-mining-a-search-for-knowledge

School of Science and Engineering

Atlantic International University

USA

Data Mining

Mohamed Ahmed Mohamed Osman Rahama

<u>January, 2012</u>

Table of Contents:

1

Introduction

The steady advancement in Information Technology (IT) as we know results in the presence of a massive data stored either in operational databases or a huge data warehouses which increases the need to develop effective tools that are characterized by speed, accuracy and intelligence in the data analysis aspect and extraction of information and knowledge. Hence the so-called Data Mining (DM) and sometimes called knowledge discovery appeared as an effective technique aimed for finding knowledge from huge amounts of data i.e. transforming such data into useful information and transforming information into knowledge. "Data mining is the analysis step of the knowledge discovery in databases process". [7]. Data mining has been emerged as a result of the development in the heterogeneous database systems in conjunction with the great development in computer hardware industry especially in storage technology. So we come for answering the questions what is data mining? And what is its importance? There are many definition of this concept which defines it simply as "mining knowledge from large amounts of data" while Jiawei Han and Micheline Kamber (2006 p.7) adopted a broad view that says "data mining is the process of discovering interesting knowledge from large amounts of data stored in databases, data warehouses, or other information repositories". So data mining is exploration in large volumes of data as well as the discovery of the relationships between them and summarized it into useful knowledge to be used in business for increasing income and reducing costs or in other words answering questions that are specialized and very wide when compared to the traditional and statistical query tools. Data mining means extracting the underlying unusual concepts which were not previously known. It is not like the traditional techniques that used for extraction of quantitative information generated by applications such as decision support systems and statistical methods in which information are specified prior to the extraction process, but it is simply the discovery of a hideout value in the data warehouse to generate predictions for future use.

The discovery of knowledge process in databases in general includes a number of stages, starting from the collection of the raw data to the stage that concerning the obtaining of new knowledge. Through this paper we will discuss data mining concepts and the data processing techniques which cover all of these stages and include data cleaning, data integration, data selection, data transformation, pattern evaluation and lastly knowledge presentation. This paper also aims to discuss the data mining concepts and study its principles and algorithms for knowledge discovery. This study will present the data mining techniques and models such as classifications, clustering, associations, description, estimation and prediction and sampling some design approach by using oracle data miner software.

Data mining main objectives

Data mining has proved its existence as one of the successful solutions for the analysis of large amounts of data and turns it from the accumulated and incomprehensible data to valuable information which can be exploited to take advantage of it as knowledge. The main objectives of using data mining, however, can be classified in the following points:

1. To explain some of observed phenomena, for example why the proportion of smokers increases in the country in the recent years?
2. To verify a theory, for example: validation of the theory which says that large families interested in health insurance rather than small families.
3. To analyze the data for new and unexpected relationships, for example: how will be the public expenditure that was inherent in the deception operations in a wide range of credit cards.

Data mining concept

Data mining is a computerized or a manual search for knowledge from huge historical data without prior assumptions about what can be defined. It is an analytical process to explore and search a huge database to extract useful patterns and relationships and to find the correlation between its elements Data mining is a new technology that enables the predictive pattern discovery, hypothesis creation and testing, and insight-provoking generation. Data mining which is also known as Knowledge Discovery in Database (KDD) is any application which has a capability for extracting hidden knowledge and it is not related to any specific industry. It is considered as one of the top ten information technology aspects that will change the world in the coming years Data mining process blends between artificial intelligence science, statistics, machine learning and databases

Why mining data?

We stand daily in long line at big supermarkets waiting for our turn to pay the value of some of our purposes which we have purchased. During this period of waiting we hear multiple beeps coming out from many barcode readers. We know that any barcode beep is a transaction, and represented by a purchase record stored in the database. So, hundred thousands of records can be accumulated in the database per day. These records, however, contain important information of purchase process for many items and also the best-selling items. But how can we benefit from all of this data and how to make it useful in our business? Data mining technology only can answer this question. The problem is not like the past concentrated in the lack of storage space and insufficient data but, in fact, our lack in the experiences that is capable to convert this data to a valuable knowledge. "It is a process that helps identify new opportunities by finding fundamental truths in apparently random data" as stated by Sumathi and Sivanandam (2006 p8).

As we said before, data mining technology is the process of extrapolation in a large volume of data in order to detect influencing factors of a particular behavior such as the causes, conditions, contraindications etc., it has abilities to perform tasks that is not found or can not be provided by the traditional applications. Data mining is not directed to a specific domain but it has a clear impact in all life aspects. So, we can summarize its importance in information industry and why we use it in the following points:

- Eextraction of useful patterns become important in light of rapid development and widespread dissemination of databases
- Its usage provides institutions and security services in all areas the ability to explore and focus on the useful and effective information in the database.

- Data mining techniques focuses on building future predictions and explore the behavior and trends and allowing assessment of the right decisions in time. Data mining techniques capable to answer complex questions in record time, especially the types of questions those has been difficult to find answers to them by using classical statistical techniques.
- Not to surrender to the limits imposed by traditional methods like statistics and numerical analysis, data mining provides the maximum benefits from the modern curriculum, such as artificial intelligence and qualitative analysis.
- Data mining helps to discover new relationships that may lead to the discovery of new theories and cooperates in science development
- Data mining provides enterprises and institutions the ability to focus on most important information in databases

The process of knowledge discovery

The discovery of knowledge in a database is a process connected with managers and decision makers who are involved in results implementation. The KDD process consists of seven stages and can be summarized as follows:

1. Data cleaning: during this phase we refine data and isolate data that contains noise, inconsistency or impurities from the data set.
2. Data integration: combining of multiple data sources, manipulating data of variable elements that may be included in a common data source.
3. Data selection: this stage is used to identify and retrieve relevant data from the data set.
4. Data transformation: is the process of transferring data that have been selected into a form suitable for search and retrieval procedures.
5. Data mining: is applications process where intelligent techniques and algorithms take place so as to gather useful data pattern.
6. Pattern evaluation: after extracting the important models of data patterns which represent the knowledge, these patterns are evaluated based on specific standards and measurements.
7. Knowledge presentation: the last stage of knowledge discovery in databases which is visual to the end user, this phase uses the basic visual technique to help the end user to understand and interpret the results of data mining.

Stages 1 through 4 represent data preprocessing procedures i.e. preparing accurate data for mining processes. Fig (1) illustrates a general overview of data mining system architecture. We notice that the data mining is only one step in KDD and it consists of complex data miner applications for knowledge extraction and the resulting knowledge may be stored further in a knowledge base. Referring to fig (1) we can say that the structure of data mining consists of six components as follows:

1. Data warehouse, flat files, database, World Wide Web or any other data storage container where the data preprocessing techniques take place.
2. Database or data warehouse server which is dealing with retrieving and capturing data according to the data mining user requests.
3. Knowledge base which is used for storing the extracted knowledge for further evaluation of the resulting patterns.

4. Data mining engine which consists of data mining applications modules that perform all data mining functions such as **classification, summarization, clustering, association rules, prediction, time series analysis, regression and sequence discovery.**
5. Pattern evaluation module which communicates with the data mining modules for measuring the interestingness and focusing the search towards interesting patterns.
6. User interface is responsible of communication between the end user and the data mining modules and provides the end user ability to perform his query tasks, perform all **exploratory data mining,** browsing databases and data warehouses and evaluate their schemas and data structures.

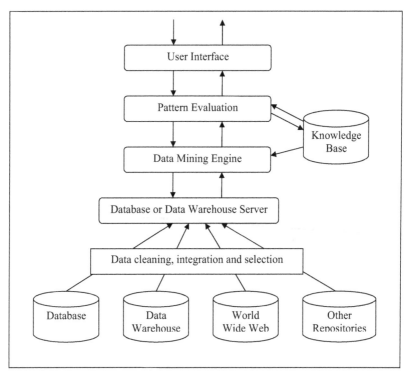

Fig (1) Data Mining System Architecture.

The KDD knowledge output can be accommodated in decision making, query processing, information management and process control. Therefore, according to **Jiawei Han and Micheline Kamber** " Data mining is considered one of the most important frontiers in database and information systems and one of the most promising interdisciplinary developments in the information technology" (2006 p10).

Data preprocessing

Data preprocessing is considered to be the very serious stage in the data mining and the correct exploration in database should be built on a data that ensures the flow of knowledge. The databases, as we know, contain groups of a very large amount of data that is collected through certain automated methods that are not completely controlled. So the databases are vulnerable to missing, incorrect, incomplete, inconsistent and noisy data which represent the inputs to analysis processes and therefore the knowledge discovery. An attention should be paid to the quality of data, if not collected and selected carefully may leads to misleading results specifically in the predictive data mining. The data preprocessing methods such as data selection, data cleaning, data integration and data transformation should be applied to the database to correct errors, remove noisy data and gathering data from various data sources. Descriptive data summarization techniques can be applied first to highlight the data properties and distinguish between noisy, missing, incorrect, outliers and incomplete data. Human data entry contributes to an inaccurate and missing data and it is data cleaning process functions to deal with the data entry errors. Data integration process is responsible for well designed schema in its tables, attributes and constraints, i.e. schema that contains no redundancies when combing data from different data sources. The data transformation process is concerned with data structure i.e. the data should be transformed and encapsulated in a form suitable for mining. The ETL software which allows extract, transform and load data to and from a database or a data warehouse play an important role in the data transformation process. Finally, data mining requires that the database or data warehouse that containing an up to date data and as Larose said "Data mining often deals with data that hasn't been looked at for years" (2005 p28).

Data mining methods

The data mining methods can be grouped into two major types: predictive data mining and descriptive data mining. Descriptive data mining such as summarization, clustering, association rules and sequence discovery deals with the general characteristics of data in the database and it depends on the reorganization of data and mining in its depths as if for the extraction of models that allows you to create a simple description of similar entities such as similar customers in sales database and no target is required for such data. The predictive data mining, on the other hand, is trying to find the best predictions based on the data, such as knowing the best and the preferred product to a specific customer. In brief, this type of data mining depends on the historical data i.e. using old information to predict or forecast for what will happen in the future. Unlike descriptive data mining, the predictive data mining has a target to achieve. The descriptive data mining tasks can be summarized in classification, regression, time series analysis and prediction. In the following paragraph we will highlight some of data mining tasks which include classification, clustering, association rule, sequence discovery, regression, and time series analysis.

1. Classification:

Classification is used widely in solving many problems, especially those tasks which are related to the business. Classification means extracting groups of information based on common properties or characteristics of group's elements such as the classification of electricity prepaid customers based on their monthly purchases or classification of thermal electricity power stations based on fuel consumption. Classification is carried out through a series of data analysis that preparing the output in the form of divisions or classes which can be used later for the future data classification and this shows the main difference between clustering and classification. There are many types of techniques that can be used in the data classification by using many of algorithms such as, statistical algorithms, neural networks, decision tree, genetic algorithms and the nearest neighbor algorithms.

2. Clustering:

Clustering in data mining is a process of dividing the data into group of records based on their participation in similar properties. In other words, the cluster is a group of similar purposes that interacts with each other, and it is similar to the members belonging to other clusters. Larose defined it as "a cluster is a collection of records that are similar to one another and dissimilar to records in other clusters" (2005 p16). Clustering technique is subdivided into two main types: distance based clustering and conceptual clustering. Distance clustering arises when two purposes or more are being close to each other according to a certain distance while the conceptual clustering means one or more purposes belong to the same cluster based on the concept of common descriptive purposes. Clustering is a division that is not directed to the data. It helps the user to understand the structure of the natural groupings of data.

3. Association rule:

Association rule is considered as one of the most promising windows of data mining. It is a knowledge discovery tool and has ability to search large data. Association rule allows capturing all possible rules that illustrate some of the characteristics that are dependent on the presence of other characteristics. In other words, are the rules of correlation between a particular set of data in the database. Examples of association rules such as investigating the proportion of cell phone company subscribers who respond to a service upgrade to company plan. Also, extracting items in a supermarket that are purchased together and items those are purchased alone. "Association rules show strong associations between attribute-value pairs (or *items*) that occur frequently in a given data set" as Jiawei Han and Micheline Kamber said (2006 p344).

4. Sequence discovery

Sequence discovery techniques searched in the database to discover the patterns that occur sequentially. The input is a set of consecutive data (form a series set), each series of data is a list of operations or terms and when the process is a group of terms it must be calculated with the time associated with each process. But the problem with this model lies in finding all sequential models with less support allocated by the user, when the support to this model is the ratio of the sequential data that contained in the pattern. The interactive sequence discovery responds quickly to each query and reduces data mining time for the whole process.

5. Regression

Regression in data mining uses the current or existing values to predict for what will be the other values. In its simple case, regression uses standard statistical techniques such as linear regression. But many of the problems in the real world are not just a linear forecast of the previous or old values. For example, in stock prices, the volume of purchases, and the rates of success or failure of a product is often difficult to predict because it may depends on very complex variables interactions which have a lot of expectations. Therefore, you may need more complex techniques such as decision tree, neural networks and logistic regression and others to forecast for future values.

6. Time series analysis

Time series analysis forecasts for future values that are unknown and this analysis is done based on a predictable series of time-varying. Time series just like regression in using known results that leading to future predictions. Time series models depend on the distinctive characteristics of time, especially in the hierarchy periods, (for example, a variety of definitions such as the working week is it five days or six days etc)., seasonal effects, calendar effects such as holidays, and other special considerations such as the past effects. Time series databases are used in sales forecasting, economic analysis, stock market studies, quality control etc.

6. Prediction

Prediction is similar to classification except that in prediction the data is classified on basis of predicting the future behavior or estimating its future value, as the dependent variable which is predicted is a quantitative variable. Examples of prediction in business such as stock pricing prediction for the next month, prediction of electricity loads and sales for the next year, and the prediction traffic death in the next six months. The new tools that used in prediction include decision tree, neural networks, nearest neighbor and genetic algorithms.

Data Mining Algorithms and Models

Data mining science in databases rose as a natural result of the exponential growth of data, especially after the widespread use of information systems which leads to an accumulation of a huge data that are traded daily in many areas, and this led to an urgent need to answer many questions that explore the knowledge and estimates and forecasts for the future. Questions that have no answers in the traditional statistical analysis such as description of the data (graphs), measures of central tendency, measures of dispersion and regression etc. Data mining, as we defined it before, **aims to explore** the knowledge hidden in the databases. Data mining operations include the analysis that using the following algorithms and models:

- Nearest neighbor algorithm.
- Clustering algorithm.
- The decision tree algorithm.

- Neural networks algorithm.
- Rule induction algorithm.

1. Nearest neighbor algorithm

The nearest neighbor algorithm is considered as data mining technique which aims to predict by comparing the similar records to the record that we want to predict for, and estimating the unknown value of this record based on the information of those records. Nearest neighbor algorithm is easy to implement and perform well in many areas and it is often used in business. Commonly used examples of nearest neighbor algorithm are algorithms those help people to purchase goods by choosing those closest to their needs rather than goods which have been already purchased.

In the security area, we can use this algorithm to detect the perpetrators of a crime by using information of similar offenses which have been committed previously to determine the identity of the perpetrator of the current crime. This is done by identifying the number of experimental or training records that used to predict the required value as defined by Jiawei Han and Micheline Kamber "Nearest-neighbor classifiers are based on learning by analogy, that is, by comparing a given test tuple with training tuples that are similar to it" (2006 p348). (In RDBMS tuples consist of attributers and it means rows or records). For example, if we have a range of crimes of a specific type that have been committed previously, the use of this algorithm will be is that to examine the situation around the nature of the criminals who are committed those types of crimes, and neighbors in this case is the basic characteristics of those criminals, such as their age, educational level and social status as well as the motives of the crime commission, but this does not negate a specific characteristic or nature of the neighborhood which was not into account, can be discovered and so leads to the disclosure of the wanted criminal. The confidence in the results of what has been reached to explore by using the nearest neighbor algorithm is very important, and we may express this by saying that we are confident 60% of a particular value of what we explored. The confidence can be determined based on:

1. The distance between the explored record and the nearest neighbor.
2. Homogeneity of the neighborhood group and whether they lead to the same explored value.

2. Clustering algorithms

Cluster analysis is the process of compiling similar records in groups, and it is designed for high level of exploration in the database. Clustering is considered as an introductory step in the process of data mining. Clustering algorithms used to build clusters such that the between-cluster variation (BCV) is large when related to the within-cluster variation (WCV). Clustering idea is like keeping or organizing books in a library where a large number of books with variety types of topics are available. In library, similar books are kept in one place. For example, computer science books kept in one cupboard and mathematics books in another cupboard. To reduce the search, further organization is applied on computer science books such as keeping the databases books in a shelf, operating system books in another shelf and so on. The main goal of clustering algorithm is to determine the grouping of unlabeled data set. Clustering algorithms are applied in many fields and should satisfy scalability, multiple and different attributes, dealing with outliers and noise, and ability to order records.

Clustering algorithms is subdivided into two types: hierarchal clustering and partitioning clustering. Hierarchal clustering is a treelike in its structure and it is created either by decomposition or splitting (divisive) methods or merging of already existing clusters which is known as combining (agglomerative) method.

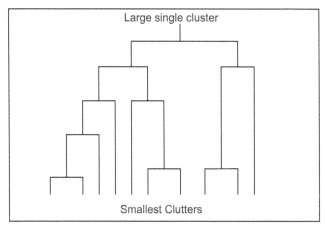

Fig (2) Hierarchal clustering structure.

Divisive method starts with big cluster searches its records and moves all dissimilar records in a separate cluster and this process continue and repeated until each record represents its cluster. Each cluster group must contain one record (tuple) and each record must belong to only one group. The combing method, however, start by observing tiny cluster then any similar clusters are merged in a new cluster. This means that any combination reduced the number of clusters by one. In brief, hierarchal clustering methods are a bottom-up approach. The impact of hierarchal method is that once a process of split or merge is done it can not rollbacks. If we considered a data set consist of {a, b, c, d, e} objects then agglomerative and divisive methods cab be demonstrated as shown in fig (3).

Partitioning methods divides the data records into portions, each partition represent a cluster. Partitioning methods starts by creating an initial partition and then using iterative relocation technique to move records between groups and improve partitioning. The major partitioning methods algorithms are k-means, k-medoids, and CLARNAS algorithms. K-means and k-medoids deal with small and medium databases while CLARNAS perform well with very large databases.

The clustering analysis can be applied in security area to fragments people or the general population into groups that can be studied directly and specifically. For example, when studying the crime rates in detail for each age group we can be concluded that the rate is less in general, but increasing for a particular age group. Also clustering analysis can be used in grouping persons

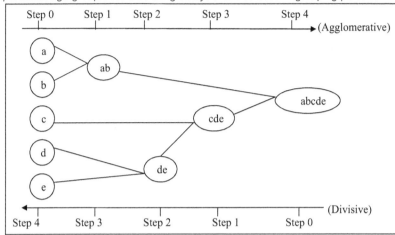

Fig (3) Agglomerative and divisive hierarchical clustering

associated with a particular issue in order to explore the links and differences that can be utilized in the decoding that issue.

3. Decision tree algorithms

According to Ian H. Witten and Eibe Frank the decision tree algorithm can be defined as "A divide-and-conquer approach to the problem of learning from a set of independent instances leads naturally to a style of representation called a decision tree" , (2005 p62). Decision tree is a model of exploratory appears as its name expresses, on the form similar to a tree, and specifically its branches represents all of the taxonomically question and leafs represent parts of the database that belonging to the classes that have been created. The decision tree contains nodes that connected by branches, its root is the top node. The node with no possibility to split in further nodes is called leaf node. Fig (4) predicts whether a customer at computer hardware company will purchase a computer or not.

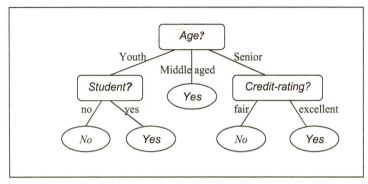

Fig (4) Decision tree sample

The decision tree, in addition to its use in the discovery of data for statistical functions, it is also used more in prediction. When building a decision tree algorithm it is extremely important to consider that the decision tree being viable as possible and ideal to all existing and available data The basic concept or criteria when building a decision tree is to put the best question at each branch of the tree so that this question divides the data into two sections, the first section contains the data of those the question applied to them and the second section to those does not apply, and thus by applying a series of questions the decision tree is built with its all branches. The learning steps of decision tree yields good accuracy. There are two types of algorithms that are used in constructing decision trees: C4.5 algorithm and Classification and regression trees (CART) algorithm. CART is binary and creates only two branches for each node while C4.5 algorithm creates more than two branches.

Lastly, we can say that the decision tree algorithms differ from clustering algorithms in the following:

- Decision tree technique aimed to split the database according to a particular goal that has already been determined
- The existence of a certain element in a branch, is a result of achieving a series of conditions that set down to this section, and not just because it looks like the rest of the elements, although there is no similarity is defined in this case.
- Decision tree may be more complex than the retail cluster, but lead to results that can be displayed in a simple and a high interest level

4. Neural Networks algorithms

Nneural networks also known as back-propagation algorithm is a learning algorithm. Neural network is a set of units that connected to each other, and each connection has a weight related to it. Neural networks combined with decision trees are classified as the most effective and commonly used methods of data mining, because of the reliability and accuracy which can be reached when those algorithms are used and it is possible to be applied for solving complex problems, this despite to the difficulty which led to non-proliferation widely for both of them.

Neural network algorithm is similar in composition to the human brain, it works the same way as the brain is working in transferring and processing information to reach conclusions and discovers patterns and predictions and they can apply some of what normal brain applies. Although scientists up to this day are still discovering more and more but they did not become familiar with all details of human brain work. According to Jiawei Han Micheline Kamber "A neural network, when used for classification, is typically a collection of neuron-like processing units with weighted connections between the units", (2006 p24). Neural network consists of nodes (which correspond to nerve cells) and the connections that link them (which resembles the neural connections).

Neural networks are built in a form of multiple layers with no feedback loops. Neural network can be used in many fields such as process control, monitoring, investment analysis, marketing, and signature analysis, toys, and voice and speech recognition. Neural networks are flexible, high accuracy, easy to maintain and independence from prior assumptions.

The following figure Fig (5) shows the construction of a simple neural network, which take the age and income variables as input and give the predictive result of whether a person will accept to commit a certain crime or an act

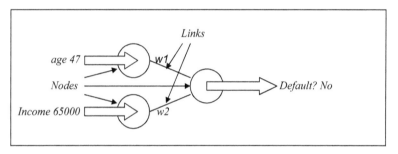

Fig (5) Simple neural network

To apply neural network for prediction, the variables known values are entered in the nodes that specified for input, and each node holds the value of the variable that was entered, then the value of each node is multiplied by the value of its related link to get the result. Neural networks could not compute attributes values in their original forms, so in stead they use indicators to handle the computation. For example, suppose a gender attribute in a data set with values male and female, for female records we can assign 0 to male and 1 to female and vice versa for male records we assign 0 to female and 1 to male i.e. the probability is ranged between 0 and 1. In general, categorical variables with n classes can be represented by n-1 indicator variables. Therefore for marital status variable with values married, separated, divorced, single, widowed, and unknown we can assign their weight values 0.0, 0.2, 0.4, 0.6, 0.8 and 1.0 respectively. The output of neural network in all cases is ranged between zero and one.

Referring to above example we expect that the person is ventured to commit the crime if the result is near to one and is considered not to respond to act if the result is near to zero. The values of nodes and weights are assigned according to the following:

- For values to be ranged between 0 and 1 we estimated 0.47 to represent the age of 47 yeas, and 0.65 to represent the income value of 65000$.
- For links (*w1 and w2*) that reflect the weights, the appreciation values are considered to be 0.7 for w1 and 0.1 for w2 and this was estimated based on knowledge of historical database records

Then, when multiplying the values of the nodes by the values of links (weights) we get the value of the variable that we want to forecast, and here it is 0.39. (0.47*0.7+0.65*0.1). So, the result is closer to zero than to one which indicates that the person is not likely to commit the crime. Numeral networks, however, are characterized by parallelism which contributes in speeds up the computation process.

Neural network algorithm may contain other types of nodes, so-called hidden nodes or layers. The main role of these nodes is advisory and its values are not taken until the adoption of consultancy in the case of passing the actual tests. The hidden layers have no direct connection to the environment and appear in the multilayer perception. The hidden layers evolve whenever the neural network algorithms are applied. The development and modernization of the original nodes takes place depending on the appropriate values of hidden nodes that support and obtain more accurate results. In contrast, the values of hidden nodes are neglected when they have not achieved any results.

5. Rule induction algorithms

Rule induction is one of basic data mining techniques and the most common in the exploration of knowledge. Rule induction is closer to the so-called mining process itself. Rule induction shows what is happening inside the database and also shows us what we did not know before and perhaps the knowledge that we can not discover unless we apply it. Induction rule is an alternative method of mining by using association rule and may be expressed by the following form:

if (*attribute a, value a*) and (*attribute b, value b*) and …. and (*attribute n, value n*) then (*decision, value*)

For example, if we apply multiple analyses on the crimes database we can explore the following rule which says: "If the offender committed the crime of type (A), he will commits the crime of type (B), with the possibility of 80%, and this duality occurs as total of 3% when compared to the total number of recorded crimes". In order to draw such a rule the database should be complete and useful and this is achieved by its accuracy percentage and its coverage. Database coverage means the proportion of records that achieved the rule compared to the total number of records in the database. To illustrate the database accuracy and converge, suppose that in a police traffic database we did multiple analyses of accidents that lead to the following rule: "If the driver has committed 10 traffic violations it commits a traffic accident that leads to the murder" and if we considered that the database contains records that classified as following manner:

T = 100, the total number of records in the database.

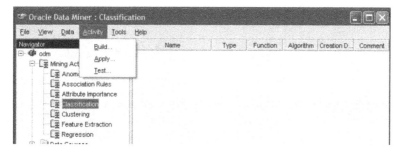

Fig (6) Oracle data miner (odminer.exe)

In this section we will discuss classification technique using decision tree algorithm and clustering techniques using k-means clustering algorithm. The following steps illustrate the data mining classification method with decision tree algorithm:

- As shown in Fig (6), we select classification from mining activities menu and from main menu we select activity followed by selection of the option build. The application wizard which contains 5 steps started and the screen as shown in fig (7) appear.
- In function type field we select classification and then we select the decision tree algorithm and proceed forward to the next screen.

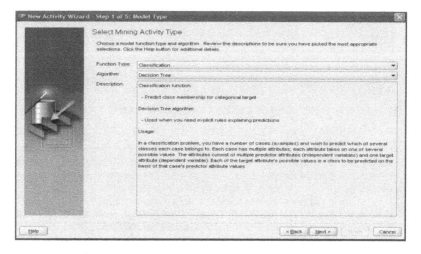

Fig (7) Selection of data mining method and algorithm

- In step 2, (data screen) we select the database schema and the database object (table/view), and then we select the table unique identifier which here is the customer ID and then proceed to step 3.
- In step 3, we select marital status as a target for the decision tree target and then proceed to step 4.

- In step 4, we select (married) as preferred target value for marital status.
- Step 5 is specified for comments and then the application starts building the pattern which depends on family size and age attributes. The results appear in 5 levels as shown in fig (8) and include the predictive confidence for each of decision tree levels.

In order to manipulate the clustering method we repeat the same above steps with minor differences limited in the targeted attribute and its value which are not included in the clustering. Among the algorithms included in this method we select k-means algorithm. Unlike the classification method, the clustering activity processes passed through several treatments, starting with sampling, outlier treatment, missing value treatment, normalization and ending with the build process.

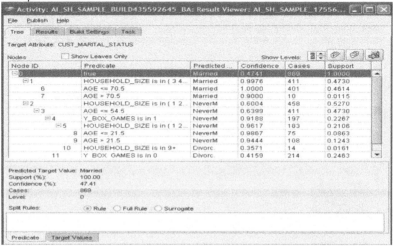

Fig (8) Decision tree algorithm output

Fig (9) shows 19 clusters in 6 cluster levels with 10 leaves and the number of cases (records) per each cluster. Fig (10) shows the clusters rules which is subdivided into two parts, the upper part consists of cluster ID, prediction percentage confidence and the support count, while the lower part shows the rule details for each cluster which is actually an if then statement.

Oracle data miner also includes a data menu which contains multiple tools like copy table, create table from view, create view, generate SQL etc Also includes data mining tools like transform, predict and explain. There also a tools menu for repository synchronization, SQL worksheet and oracle PL/SQL developer.

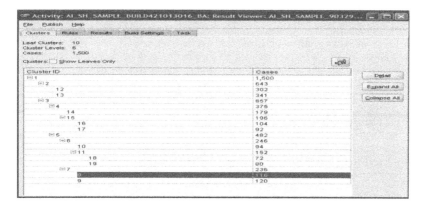

Fig (9) Clustering technique and algorithm output

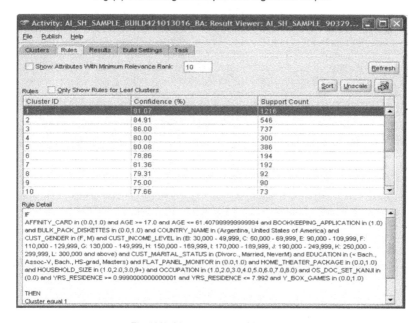

Fig (10) Clustering algorithm rules

Mining the WEB

There is no doubt that with the beginning of this century, the numbers of WEB sites have increased dramatically, and the information available on the internet has become tremendous and even exhaustive. The WEB sites became common for enterprises, institutions, and even persons in the majority of countries, including developing ones. There have been huge databases, blogs, encyclopedias and documents, which had a significant impact on the internet

18

search engines. The search engines, however, faltered in finding the required information from all of these frightening quantities of data to a point where a an internet researcher became as one who cast the net in the sea, captures the simple things and leave the valuable ones in the depths. Search engines have evolved a lot, and the researcher is no longer limited to the selection of keywords or the topic when he use these engines, but the researcher had become, through specific lists narrow the search by choosing a part of network or the entire network, Also he can choose the country, the language, the period and application instructions regarding the search or what is called transactional logic, such as coupling between the words and use of parentheses, quotation marks, the star and others. However, we find a lot of researchers stumble to find lots of the required information, such as: blogs, books and articles which leads to boredom and drive the researcher to go back to the old methods. Therefore, the thinking is directed to solve this problem in order to help access the treasures hidden in the Internet, and this was achieved by evolving a new technique called mining the WEB.

The WEB is the most largest and open publishing system which contains hundred millions of sites of all data types format. Mining the WEB means applying data mining methods such as classification rules and grouping of users according to their interest, to a variety of data structures, forms and patterns of data contained in the World Wide Web. Data mining the WEB depends, basically, on how all types of WEB documents are collected and indexed and this is a key factor for searching processes. The WEB data increases significantly every day which make the searching for a document in the internet sometimes worst and very difficult for end users. The internet documents are accessed through URL links and mainly the user follow a sequence of linked documents organized in hierarchical structures to reach his target. Many searching engines like Yahoo, Google and others are available to assist us to reach our targets by using a set of words or keywords, but the question that arises is that how to turn this huge amount of data into what we can say, WEB knowledge. I think this can be achieved either by applying new intelligent searching techniques or changing the structure of web pages. Semantic WEB is a new technology which helps to bring the techniques of knowledge discovery into the WEB. The web consortium www.w3c.org offers comprehensive information about the most modern WEB knowledge developments or semantic WEB.

The development of new techniques concerning WEB mining or in other words, the emergence of more effective search engines, will help to alleviate the challenges facing the WEB and all those concerned by it. It will also give it intelligence, make it more acceptable, encourage most of people to support and use it positively for discovering the real knowledge, and help them to make the appropriate decisions which lead to achieve the desired objectives and success

Advantages and disadvantages of data mining

Data mining become of great importance in today's technology to assist in discovering interesting patterns which are unknown from large databases. The main advantages of data mining can be summarized in the following:

1. Data mining applications are interactive, well-performing, understandable, visual, and connected directly to databases, data marts and data warehouses.

19

2. The discovery of the hidden knowledge that can not be discovered by using traditional applications.
3. Data mining, in business, provides business with actual and accurate trends about customer purchasing behaviors.
4. Data mining, in law enforcement, assists enforcers to identify criminal's suspects and examining trends about their habits, location, crime type etc.
5. Data mining play an important role in e-commerce trends and electricity demands and supply analysis.
6. Provides answers to the complex and unresolved questions those can not be resolved by using traditional query tools.

Although, data mining is considered to be one of today's leading technology but it has some disadvantages that can be summarized in the following:

1. Some of data mining tools are difficult to understand by business analysts or users.
2. Privacy issues leads people to be afraid of their personal information is collected and used in immoral way that causing some trouble.
3. There is a security issue problem concerning private data, for example employees or customers personal information will be vulnerable and exposed to hackers.
4. Misuse of data collected in databases by unauthorized users.

Data mining future

Data mining future trends is directed towards predictive analytics to achieve customer satisfaction that appears as a result of intensive competition between companies. The emergence of market for predictive analytics should be secured by professional services. Our vision for data mining future is to search for patterns in data and to develop algorithms that capable to manipulate very complex objects such as strings, graphs, pictures and movies. Data preprocessing is an important phase in data mining process and it has a clear impact on results obtained by data mining algorithms; data mining future should take into account the development and promotion of the methods used in data preprocessing to include complex data objects. Data preprocessing phase should be automated to be faster, transparent and more powerful than today. Data mining applications should be developed to include all possible algorithms that have ability to increase data mining usability and to generate variety types of complex pattern that can be easily interpreted.

Conclusion

The growing need of enterprises for fast analytical results, intense competition, the rapid changes in the work environment, the enormous development in the data storage methods and the emergence of data warehouses make data mining and knowledge discovery by using modern methods is the biggest challenge for all institutions and corporations.

Data mining is a tool that is used to discover the knowledge that is unknown to us, and to predict and specify trends of purposes which are in our minds. The integration of information technology advantages with statistical methods and algorithms to provide the necessary capabilities to predict the behavior of the future and then develop the appropriate solutions to problems before they occur, or in general, a matter of prediction for development and modernization in various fields uses the data mining techniques to explore more comprehensive knowledge in databases. Data mining has become one of the major concerns for all countries and institutions.

The electricity supply industry is the function of the corporation where I work. It is very important for all electricity utilities to predict for future demand for electricity power early as possible. Optimal estimates for minimum and maximum loads per each hour, day, week, month, season and year has a great economic values for our electricity companies to set maintenance scheduling, operating reserve, fuel supply and spare parts inventory management. Load Dispatch Center LDC is a nerve of power system that ensures secure and safe grid operation. LDC uses may applications for electricity grid management such as Supervisory Control and Data Acquisition (SCADA) system is a computerized system which capturing a huge of operational data that concerning the grid components and status daily. I hope that data mining techniques being implemented in analyzing this data for optimal Load forecasting and demand estimation instead of using classical applications.

In my country I hope that people work on planning and building strategic databases and data warehouses to help in good analysis and enhance the possibility of coordination and cooperation between the various institutions to share their data in order to construct databases that satisfy knowledge discovery.

References

1. Han, Jiawei. Kamber, Micheline. *Data Mining: Concepts and Techniques*. Second Edition, (2006). Elsevier Inc.

2. Larose, Daniel. *Data Mining Methods and Models.* (2006). *John* Wiley & Sons, INC Publication.

3. Larose, Daniel. *Discovering Knowledge in Data: An Introduction to Data Mining*, (2005). *John* Wiley & Sons, INC Publication.

4. Witten, Ian. Frank, Eibe. *Data Mining: Practical Machine Learning Tools and Techniques*, Second Edition (2005). Elsevier Inc.

5. Zdravco, Markov. Larose, Daniel. *Data Mining the WEB: Uncovering Patterns in Web Content, Structure, and Usage*.(2007). John Wiley & Sons, INC Publication.

6. http://en.wikipedia.org/wiki/Data_mining .

7. http://docs.oracle.com/cd/B28359_01/datamine.111/b28130.pdf .

www.ingramcontent.com/pod-product-compliance
Lightning Source LLC
Chambersburg PA
CBHW031234050326
40689CB00009B/1604